EMOTIONAL INTELLIGENCE

Raise Your EQ (Mastering Self Awareness & Controlling Your Emotions

EDWARD BENEDICT

Contents

Introduction

Congratulations on purchasing this book and thank you for doing so.

We all know that letting our emotions run high is never a good thing. The last time you saw someone have an emotional outburst in public, how did that make you feel? Did you perceive them positively or negatively?

Whether you're extremely happy, you feel like you could jump through the roof right now, or feeling so angry that you could punch a hole through a wall, there's one thing that is a common factor in both scenarios. Being overly emotional is never good. Ever.

Emotions have a way of taking control over you to a point where you lose all sense of rationality. You can't think straight, you react impulsively, and worst of all, you could find yourself saying things you don't mean which end up hurting people around you. Reacting and speaking emotionally is perhaps the most dangerous thing of all. Once something has been said and done, it can never be undone. That is perhaps the most damaging thing to a relationship you could do.

Feeling extremely happy or angry is never a good idea. Even being extremely happy, for example. When you're running on an emotional high, it's easy to let your perception and judgment be clouded. How many times have you made an impulsive decision on a happy high, only to regret that decision later once the euphoria has gone? Likewise, it is also an equally bad idea to react when you're in an emotionally angry state. How many times have you found yourself saying things you immediately regret once the anger has dissipated?

Emotional Intelligence, also known as EQ, is not like the intelligence you're normally accustomed to when you hear the word *intelligent*. It isn't about being academically brilliant. It is about intelligent, yes, but *emotionally* instead of academically. Being book smart is great, but they can only get you so far in life. To achieve true success in every aspect, you're going to need to master this very crucial skill which often doesn't get enough credit as it should.

EQ is a form of intelligence which can guide all of us to make better decisions. Emotions can be more powerful than you can imagine. Without the proper tools and management techniques, you can easily find yourself overwhelmed and at a loss for what to do. Uncontrolled emotions can leave a tremendously powerful impact on your life. A classic example would be how uncontrolled emotions lead to feelings of depression and anxiety; two very real conditions which exist because of a person's inability to manage their emotions properly.

While EQ may not entirely be the cause of depression and anxiety, it certainly is a contributing factor. People who suffer from those two conditions often find themselves feeling so overwhelmed by their emotions that they completely shut down and retreat into themselves. They feel crippled, they feel despair, and everything in life seems much harder or nearly impossible because they feel hopeless.

This is a precise example of why it is so important to learn how to manage your emotions. To control your EQ matters more when it comes to achieving success than IQ does, believe it or not. No matter how brilliant you may be academically, nobody is going to follow a leader who lets their emotions run amok. To be considered a true success, you need to master EQ. It is a skill which is going to transform your life.

Which brings us to why you're reading this book right now; because you're realizing how crucial it is to learn how to manage and understand your emotions. *Emotional Intelligence* is a guidebook which is going to help you master self-awareness by learning how to control your emotions. This is going to be a very crucial step as you now move forward to take control of both your emotional and mental wellbeing.

Emotional Intelligence is going to explore what it means to possess high EQ, how to master and control your emotions, turn your attention within and start to live a life where your emotions don't run your day.

There are plenty of books on this subject on the market, so thanks again for choosing this one! Every effort was made to ensure it is full of as much useful information as possible. Please enjoy!

What Is Emotional Intelligence

E motions. They can be a very powerful force in our lives.

Because it is so powerful that it makes *emotional intelligence* one of the most valuable assets we could cultivate for ourselves. Emotional intelligence is simply the ability to identify, manage and regulate your own emotions. It is also about being able to identify the emotions of others around you, and what you do with that information you receive. Emotional intelligence is about your ability to capitalize on these emotions and use them to your best advantage.

Emotional intelligence is often also referred to as EQ or EI.

It was a term which was first introduced by John Mayer and Peter Salavoy, who were two researchers at the time. This term was later brought to popularity by Dan Goleman, who wrote a book in 1996 with the same name.

The 5 Core Principles of Emotional Intelligence

Emotional intelligence can essentially be summed up in two ways - the ability to recognize, understand and manage your emotions, and the ability to influence the emotions of others. In Goleman's book, he divided emotional intelligence into five core principles:

- Self-awareness
- Self-regulation
- Motivation
- Empathy
- Social skills

These five core principles are the qualities that everyone with high EQ should possess. This is going to be the framework that you are going to work towards as you work on mastering self-awareness and controlling your emotions.

· · ·

Self-Awareness

How aware are you about the state of your emotions? Do you recognize them as they happen? Or do you only notice how emotional you were after you've had some time to look back and reflect on your actions? As you learn to master self-awareness, EQ is going to teach you how to recognize your emotions as they happen, how to tune in and be mindful towards what you're experiencing. EQ will teach you how to recognize the effects that your emotions have, and what to do about them.

Self-Regulation

Having an awareness of your emotions alone is not going to be enough. It is *what you do with them* that matters just as much. Are you going to let your emotions control you? Or are you going to be the one who is in control? It is easy to lose control when you don't know how to regulate your emotions, especially when they first happen. This is why self-regulation is an important step in the EQ process because it teaches you to be adaptable and flexible in handling changes. It teaches you to take responsibility for your actions, and it helps keep you in check, so you don't give in to your disruptive impulses.

Motivation

Motivation is what gives you a sense of achievement to keep on pushing forward. To constantly push yourself to be even better. To strive for high levels of excellence and to have the initiative needed to act on opportunities that present them-selves. These are qualities which are displayed by a lot of successful and influential leaders. Do you notice how they always have the optimism needed to keep pursuing their goals despite the curveballs and challenges that life throws at them? That's because they've got high levels of emotional intelligence. It keeps them going to accomplish the task and the goals that they have committed themselves to while remaining optimistic in the process. They never think about quitting because they have trained their minds always to see things from a positive perspective. They've trained them-selves to see the silver lining in every situation, and they have reprogrammed their minds to focus on solving the problem at hand.

Empathy

Empathy helps emotionally intelligent individuals recognize and anticipate the needs of another individual. They then use this ability to work on fostering and building powerful relationships with a diverse group of people. Because they have the capacity to identify the needs and wants of another person, they can decipher the feelings of others, sometimes even preventing conflict before it happens because they can sense what's brewing underneath the surface. The more you can decipher the feelings of people, the better you can manage the thoughts and approaches you send them.

Social Skills

Emotionally intelligent people make such successful leaders because they are able to inspire and guide groups of individuals. They have the ability to develop good interpersonal skills, and it is these people skills which allow them to negotiate, understand and empathize with others. Their social skills help them to form meaningful bonds with a diverse group of people, especially in a work environment. They can easily influence others with their effective, persuasive techniques. They are seen as a catalyst for change because they have developed their social skills to a point where they are seen as influential and likable individuals.

These five core principles are the reason why emotionally intelligent people are so successful at what they do. This is how they rise to the top, to become the affluent leaders that others look up to. It isn't a skill that they were born with. It is a skill that they cultivate for themselves over time and practice. EQ is a skill that you too, are going to learn to master by the time you reach the end of this guidebook.

The Qualities of People with High Emotional Intelligence

It isn't just academic intelligence that runs the world we live in. In fact, it takes a combination of several factors and intelligence types to accomplish true success — one of them is emotional intelligence. The term that is used to measure a person's intelligence is called the *quotient.*

. . .

Some examples of quotients include IQ (*intelligence quotient*), which is focused on one's ability to memorize and retrieve information from memory and logical reasoning which is also known as being academically brilliant. The emotional quotient (*EQ or emotional intelligence*) on the other hand, is focused on one's ability to manage, understand and recognize not just their own emotions, but the emotions of the people around them too.

Our emotions make up a large part of who we are. We are emotional, and sometimes we respond according to those emotions. We even make decisions based on those emotions. Having emotional intelligence is just as important - if not more- to a person's success. Not only will you be able to manage and regulate your own emotions, but you can learn to influence the minds of the people around you too, as you learn to master and become better at EQ.

It is easy to spot someone with high EQ, and if there are people around you that you can use as examples of what to strive for, that's going to be a big help. Essentially, when someone displays any of the following qualities below, it is a safe bet to say that they've got high levels of emotional intelligence:

- **They Have a High Sense of Self-Awareness -** A person with high EQ has a very clear idea of how they perceive themselves, and how others around them perceive them. Someone with high EQ has mastered the art of self-awareness to the point that they completely understand themselves and how they work. They understand what factors trigger their emotions and they have learned how to manage themselves in the most proactive manner possible. They are also not afraid to seek out honest feedback from others, and they welcome constructive criticism because it helps them develop a better understanding of themselves.

- **They've Emphatic Towards Others -** A person with high EQ has the ability to relate to the people around them in a way that many others do not. They have a strong sense of empathy, and they use that quality to see things from another person's perspective. To truly understand how someone feels, you need to be able to *walk a mile in their shoes,* as the saying goes. This quality is exactly what helps them mirror someone else's emotions and feelings, to feel what they feel. It enables them to understand what the person is going through emotionally. This is a skill which they have cultivated through practice and experience.

- **They Are Curious Creatures -** They are always on the lookout for ways they can improve, and they're ever ready to learn something new. Curiosity is one of the key traits that you need to achieve success because successful people never stop learning and growing. They are passionate about life and knowledge, and they are driven every day to look for ways to become a better version of themselves. People with high EQ are always curious, and this leads to them never wanting to stop learning.

- **Their Mind Works in Analytical Ways -** People with high EQ don't just receive information and leave it at that. On the contrary, what they do instead is process and analyze the information that they receive on a deeper level. Emotionally intelligent individuals are deep thinkers, and they are always analyzing how information can be improved on and what could be done better. This is part of what makes them such great leaders, to begin with. They are problem solvers, and they always think about the *why* behind a certain action. They think about *what* benefit that course of action brings, and if this is the best scenario for everyone involved.

- **They Think Positive -** This isn't just another cliche saying for emotionally intelligent individuals. In fact, they are the living embodiment of this aspect. Despite the obstacles and challenges that come their way, those who possess high EQ maintain an optimistic attitude because they know how important it is for the mind to maintain this level of positivity. If they allow themselves to wallow in self-pity and let themselves be consumed by negative emotions and desires, they know it is only a matter of time before things quickly spiral out of control, as it often does when negativity takes over. Being optimistic and positive is the only way to keep increasing the opportunities and improve the relationships that come their way constructively and productively.

2

How to Master Self-Awareness

Experiencing an emotion in excess is never a good thing. When something is experienced in excess, it makes it that much easier for you to feel overwhelmed and on the brink of losing control. Even excessive amounts of happiness is not a good thing, because that euphoria and happiness can result in you making decisions you normally would not.

Which brings us to why it is important to master self-awareness, becoming more self-aware of your emotional reactions is part and parcel of becoming more emotionally conscious. When you're actively mindful and aware, you become more attuned to your needs. Eventually, you'll start to develop the ability to tune into someone else's emotions too, because you're able to recognize these emotions as they are happening.

Self-Awareness Is the First And Most Important Core Principle

Because managing your emotions starts with you. Nobody can help you learn how to manage and regulate your own emotions; it has to come from within which is why the path towards developing a greater level of emotional intelligence begins with self-awareness, the first and perhaps most important core principle of EQ as a whole. Before you can move onto the next four principles, you *must* master self-awareness. Think of it in this context, if you're not *aware* that there is a problem, how would you begin fixing it? When you're not aware of what's going on with you, how would you know what the best way to regulate your actions are?

Self-awareness is going to require that you make the connection between the part of your brain that *thinks* and the part of your brain that *feels* so that you're not driven by one extreme or the other. It prevents you from acting out impulsively, and more importantly, it saves you from doing something that you may regret several hours later.

. . .

There's a reason why leaders somehow appear to have the ability to remain as cool as a cucumber, even in the most stressful of times. That's not to say they aren't experiencing any emotional turmoil within; it just means they are *aware* of the way that they feel, and they are regulating their responses to manage the situation better. Anyone who aspires to become a leader must learn to possess self-awareness, or it is never going to work.

Like everything else about emotional intelligence, self-awareness is a skill which you can learn, develop and exercise on until you get better at it. Imagine self-awareness is a brand-new muscle which you have discovered within your body, and to work on making that muscle stronger, you need to constantly exercise it until it gets better over time.

How to Start Mastering Self-Awareness

This is going to happen in stages. As you work towards mastering your self-awareness, remember to be patient with yourself every step of the way, and don't rush through the process.

Phase One

The first stage of the process is going to require that you start monitoring yourself daily. From the moment you wake up, until the time you go to bed, keep checking in with yourself. Observe the things, people or situations that tend to trigger your emotions, and ask yourself *why* this is the case.

As you feel each emotion, write it down and then assess what triggered this emotion. Write down how this particular emotion made you feel, and what you were tempted to do when it occurred. Get a little notebook that you can carry around with you and write down each emotion as you feel it pop up. Next, ask yourself if this emotion was worth the time, effort and energy you spent on it. Doing this regularly helps you get to know yourself and your triggers much better.

Phase Two

The second phase of the process towards mastering self-awareness is an exercise that is going to require you to *step outside yourself*. Imagine you're viewing yourself from an outsider's perspective. What important roles do you play in your life on a daily basis? How many people rely on you? How do you think others perceive you? In this second phase, meditation is a tool that is often helpful. Meditation requires you to reconnect with yourself, mind, body, and soul. It helps you find your focus, feel centered and feel more connected to your surroundings in a way you've never had before. Finding a quiet spot for you to meditate daily. If you can't manage this daily, contemplating several times a week would be good enough to start. Meditation is a great tool to help you feel centered emotionally again, teaching you to practice feelings of calm and learning to let go of all the stress you may have encountered during the day.

Learn to observe your emotions without judgment, assess them for what they are. Analyze them and what triggered them without being too harsh on yourself. This is an exercise for you to become aware of your current emotional state, and what triggered it. That is all.

Phase Three

Next, you'll move onto the third phase of the process, where you begin to evaluate your values. For example, as you spent time analyzing your emotions and triggers from phase one, are you spending your time wisely in the way that you react to those emotions? If you let those emotions consume you, why? Was it worth exerting that much energy and effort over it? Is the way that you're reacting based on those emotions in line with your current beliefs and values? If they aren't then why do you keep doing it?

By this stage, hopefully, you are more attuned to your emotions and able to write them down as they are happening. If you have no time to reflect on them there and then, that's okay, write down the emotions and come back later and analyze it.

Assessing your emotions and defining its causes and triggers are going to require that you spend several minutes daily just by yourself and your thoughts. Find a quiet space in your home that is free from distractions, and take a few moments to sit down and begin reflecting on everything that went on today and how it made you feel. Spending some quiet reflection time alone is important towards developing your self-awareness because it forces you to go into your mind and face your emotions instead of ignoring them or blocking them out; especially, if they happen to be unpleasant emotions. Part of becoming more self-aware is being able to confront exactly why you find yourself in such an emotional state. What is causing your distress and why do you have difficulty managing it sometimes?

Phase Four

Our lives are so busy, constantly on the go that there barely seems enough time to get in touch with ourselves. Or to even make time for ourselves for that matter. But if you are to become more self-aware, you *must make the time* to get in touch with your feelings. Not just get in touch with them, but truly understand where they are coming from. Life can sometimes seem so busy and overwhelming that it can be tempting to sweep things under the rug and not have to deal with them at all.

Remember that little notebook you were carrying around you from Phase One? That's why you need to carry it around with you. So that when you need it, whip it out and immediately write down your emotions are you identify them. If you feel joy, write it down. If you feel sadness, write it down. If you feel stress, write it down. If you feel agitation, write it down. Absolutely anything that you're feeling, write it down. Keep an emotional journal of your daily life, which you can later reflect on at the end of the day. This is the best tool to develop self-awareness because when you're writing something down, it forces you to think about and reflect on it, to consciously think about it and acknowledge its presence.

Document your emotions and feelings throughout the week. At the end of each week, start on a fresh page of your notebook or journal, and separate that page into two columns. One column is for your emotions listed throughout the week, and the other column is for the context that resulted in this emotion. Dividing them into two columns like this makes it easier for you to analyze what's going on. How many emotions did you feel this week that were positive? How many were negative? Which emotions do you think dominated the way that you felt? What caused such a reaction with you? Remember not to repress or try to ignore any emotion, especially the unpleasant ones; it is important that you be as brutally honest with yourself as possible if you want to master self-awareness and develop a deeper level of emotional intelligence.

3

The Art of Controlling Your Emotions

One of the first few things you must do for yourself in your efforts to become more emotionally intelligent is to make a personal commitment. Commit to yourself that from now on, you're no longer going to dwell on past emotional mistakes or failures. Commit to yourself that from now on, you're only going to look forward and towards improvement. Commit to doing the things you know you must do to become better.

As part of this commitment, you will not allow yourself to make excuses to justify your behavior when you do have an emotional outburst. Yes, this is going to be challenging. And yes, it is going to require some self-discipline to stick to the commitments you've made. But becoming more emotionally intelligent is just as much about the process and the journey to get there, not just about the result alone.

It is about the small changes you make daily that progress you forward, which will help you become more emotionally intelligent. Fix a routine for yourself that works and stick to it every day as best you can. Make it a habit of writing in your emotional journal at least once or several times a day.

Robert Collier couldn't have said it better himself when he uttered the phrase *success is the sum of small efforts which are repeated day in and day out.* This is what you're going to do for yourself now, slowly cultivate habits which are going to help increase your EQ levels as you move forward. Learning to control your emotions is going to be one of the hardest things to do. You're trying to learn how to control a powerful force within you, and it is going to take immense self-awareness, self-regulation, and willpower to be able to pull it off successfully.

The Art of Controlling Your Emotions Starts with You

The art of controlling your emotions first starts with your commitment to change. You have to *want* to see change, *desire* to make that change happen. That's the only way you're going to give this your 100% effort. You need to want to become a person with higher EQ because you know it is the only way you're going to achieve the success you envision for yourself. When you commit to change who you are, you're mentally preparing yourself to take the necessary action needed. You're dedicating f yourself to making this change for the better. For a successful and sustainable change, you need this level of commitment.

This is going to be what fuels your desire to master all the five core principle levels required for high EQ. This is what fuels your desire to take the next step, to keep things ongoing and to always look for solutions whenever there's a problem.

How to Start Making That Personal Commitment to Change

Begin by asking yourself why is it important to you to make this change? To develop a higher EQ? Why am I committing myself to this journey? You must be able to answer the fundamental question of *why you're doing this,* or you may find yourself lost along the way then things get challenging. Knowing your *why* is how you remind yourself to keep moving forward. Especially during the most difficult moments. When you have a clear reason for doing what you're doing, you're never in any doubt, and you always know why you must persevere.

Controlling your emotions is something that requires a deep commitment from you. This is going to be what engages you to change and to be able to maintain this change for the rest of your life.

Commit to learning how to control your emotions by following these guidelines below:

- **Have a Clear Purpose -** Make a focus list of the aspects you would like to change. For example, if anger is something you want to work on controlling first, make that your first point of focus or if it is anxiety, or nervousness, or excessive happiness for example. Any emotion that you think you would like to choose on focus controlling first. When your purpose is clear, you're less likely to lose sight of your goals.

- **Start Small -** Trying to do too much too soon is

often how we find ourselves stumbling and falling along the way. While there's a wide range of emotions that you would like to control, start with one at a time and work your way up from there. Once you've mastered one, then move onto the next one. Take it one step at a time; this isn't a race to the finish line. Take as much time as you need, as long as you successfully learn how to control your emotions at the end of the day, that's all that matters.

- **Reflect On Your Progress -** Make time for reflecting and to assess just how far you've progressed. Have your efforts been working well so far? If not, what needs to be changed? Reflection gives you a chance to pinpoint the success of your efforts thus far, and it gives you a chance to look back and see how far you've come from where you were.

- **Take a Moment to Express Yourself Freely -** The art of controlling your emotions is not just about suppressing everything that you're feeling, keeping it locked inside. Suppressing one's emotions is just as bad as being overly expressive with them. Take a moment whenever you need to find a quiet space away from everyone else where you can freely express all the emotions you feel you need to let out. Let it out, take a deep breath, get it off your chest and feel better. Once you feel much better, you can rejoin the rest of the world again.

- **Stick To It -** Follow through, no matter how difficult or challenging it may be. Change is never the easiest process in the world, but as long as you keep moving forward, the hardest part of the process will soon be behind you. Never stop trying to learn how to control your emotions, because it won't be long before you've mastered the art of doing so, as long as you keep trying. No matter how hard it gets, remember why you're doing this and the commitment that you made to yourself. Stick to it and follow through.

Surround Yourself with Emotionally Intelligent People

Success is contagious. If you want to become an emotionally intelligent person you desire, you need to start surrounding yourself with those who have already succeeded in mastering the qualities of EQ. The company that you keep has a way of influencing and rubbing off on you which is why successful individuals always preach about being careful who you let into your life, to get rid of those who hold you back and to only surround yourself with positive, like-minded individuals.

It might be time to take a good, hard look at the current company that fills your life right now. Family, friends, and colleagues. Are these people who inspire you? Are they successful role models that you could emulate? More importantly, are they emotionally intelligent individuals that you could learn from? When you spend time with the right kind of people, you will subconsciously start to mimic the things that they do. You'll find yourself observing their every action, every movement, and slowly, you'll start to include these traits and habits into your own life. Do you know any emotionally intelligent people that you could start spending your time with? Time to start spending more time with them.

Get yourself a mentor with high EQ even, someone who will be more than happy to guide you through the process of becoming a more emotionally intelligent person yourself. Getting a mentor is one of the best things you can do for yourself because these will be individuals who have already been through the journey and have reached the point that you want to be. Learning directly from them is one of the best better mindset habits you can adopt. Who better to spend your time around than with someone you look up to who can teach you what else you need to do to improve. Find someone whom you admire, preferably one that you regularly see to make it easier to stay in contact. Make it a habit of meeting regularly and plucking their pearls of wisdom.

Surrounding yourself with people who want to achieve the same goal as you can make you do things you otherwise will not do. Successful people recognize that change is inevitable and that it must take place. Unsuccessful people will begrudge the changes in you whereas successful people will be glad that it happened and welcome it. Remember how emotionally intelligent people are always curious? Because they constantly seek out new ways of improving and reinventing themselves? They never settle, and they never get complacent, they're always motivated to be better. They welcome to chance to improve, and they never shy away from a challenge.

With willpower, determination, consistency, and perseverance, becoming a master controlling your emotions is yours for the taking. Developing the art of controlling your emotions needs to become a part of your life, not just something you do as a once off. Whether you're looking to improve your personal or professional life or both, the way that you handle yourself and control your emotions makes a huge difference in the way that people view and perceive you. Do you want them to view you as an emotional liability? Or someone with leadership qualities because of how well you manage to stay calm under pressure?

4

Turning Your Attention Within

Do you notice how your mood elevates when your favorite some comes on the radio? Or that feeling of excitement when you smell something delicious cooking. What about the way your heart races in nervous anticipation as you're about to take the stage and make a big speech in front of a large audience? It requires your attention to tune into the way that your body responds and reacts to different scenarios and situations. When the attention is focused on what's happening internally, that is known is turning your attention inwards.

Scientists believe that your attention involves the prefrontal cortex of the brain. It is this part of the brain which is unique and what makes us human because it is the prefrontal cortex that is responsible for a lot of the complex and unique thoughts which occur in your brains.

When we think of having to focus our attention on something, a lot of the times, we often look outside ourselves for this to happen. We look for something external which we can focus our attention on. Whether it is a family member, friend, a show on TV you're watching, the long task list as work you need to attend to, these are all examples of external factors which we focus our attention on. Very rarely do we consider turning our attention inwards, tapping into our emotions and the way that we feel. Turning our attention inwards is something we should probably work on doing more often because it is our internal workings that determine the way that we feel, our happiness or sadness, the amount of stress that we feel and more.

Emotionally intelligent people are able to turn their attention inward through self-awareness, which is why they often respond differently to certain situations. For example, where one person could feel annoyed and angrier by the minute being stuck in traffic, an emotionally intelligent person is still able to remain calm, cool and collected, perfectly happy and content with being in the present moment.

. . .

The demanding lives that we lead require a lot of our attention to be focused outwards that we forget turning our attention inwards is just as much of a priority. It is because we don't pay enough attention to what's happening within us that we find ourselves being overwhelmed by emotions, sometimes experiencing outbursts and losing control. Our emotions have a way of creeping up on us and taking us by surprise. We may think we have everything under control, but all it takes is one trigger for the emotional floodgates to be unleashed.

Where to Begin - How to Work on Turning Your Attention Within

Our emotions can be our own worst enemy. If we let it get out of control, they can pull us down in unimaginable ways and threaten every chance we have of wanting to achieve success. The reason that you may not yet have the level of emotional intelligence you desire is that learning to listen to your emotions is something that is entirely new to you. Nobody taught you that this was a crucial life skill that you need to master. In fact, most of the time people are dismissive of their emotions, either choosing to suppress them entirely or deny them altogether. Some may even have convinced themselves that emotions are nothing but a liability, designed to slow you down and prevent you from making the cold, hard decisions that you sometimes need to.

. . .

How often have you found yourself apologizing for your reactions and outbursts because your "emotions got the best of you." Living with the guilt of those actions is not a burden you want to be carrying around for the rest of your life. Once something has been said and done, that's all there is to it. It can never be undone, and the words that have been spoken can never be forgotten. This is why you constantly need to work hard at maintaining control over one of the most powerful forces going on within you.

Learning to turn your attention inwards is a skill that needs to be learned through practice. Use the following strategies to help you practice learning how to listen to your emotions and improve your self-awareness:

- **Put a Name to Your Feelings -** Noticing your feelings alone is just one part of the process. Don't notice the way that they make you feel physically, but give them a name so you can identify with them even better. Friendly, happy, proud, nervous, angry, upset, disappointed, and thrilled are just some of the names you could give the emotions that you're feeling. Put them in a sentence and say *This makes me feel proud* or *This makes me thrilled.* Clearly defining your emotions is how you train yourself to focus on pulling your attention inwards, to where it matters the most.

- **Keeping Tabs on One Emotion a Day -** Pick an emotion a day and make it a point to keep tabs on it throughout the day. Whenever you notice the emotion happening, make a note of it or write it down in your emotional journal about the level of intensity you experience that emotion today. For example, if the emotion of your choice for today is happiness, keep tabs on it for the whole day. How often did it happen? Was the feeling strong and intense? Or just a mild passing sensation. The more detailed you are, the more attention it is going to require from you to properly focus on describing your emotions as accurately as possible.

- **Reframing the Way You Think -** Your emotions have a lot to do with the way that you perceive certain situations and events. For example, if you're already feeling nervous and worried, getting an email from your boss saying that they want to see you might aggravate your emotions even further.

You may perceive it as bad news, that you're about to be told off for a mistake that you made. Perhaps even fired. You'd probably be envisioning all the worst possible scenarios. Now, if you were to receive that same email from your boss, but you were feeling happy or jubilant that day, you'd perceive the situation in a whole different life. You might think that your boss wants to discuss a new opportunity, or give you some great feedback. Maybe even promote you. This is the perfect example to illustrate just how big of an influence our emotions can have on the way that we perceive things, and why it is important to start focusing on what's going on internally within you. Being able to identify your emotions makes it easier to reframe your thoughts by viewing situations from a realistic perspective. Does the situation warrant such an emotional reaction? Or are you letting your emotions get the best of you again?

- **Create Different Responses to Different Scenarios -** This is a little practice in self-regulation too. Think about all the times in the past where you may not have had the best reaction to certain situations because your judgment was impaired by your emotions. If faced with a similar situation again in the future, how would you handle things differently and why? Practice listing out all the different responses and reactions you would have, and ask yourself if this is what an emotionally intelligent person would do? How well are you regulating your reactions to these challenging emotional situations? You're not dwelling on the past, but rather using these past experiences as lessons which you can learn from. Observing what didn't work in the past, so you don't repeat those same mistakes in the future.

The more you notice and become aware of your emotions, the better your self-awareness skills will become. Noticing them, and accepting them for what they are is how you successfully self-regulate and determine the best course of action for yourself — one where your emotions no longer get the best of you.

5

Living a More Positive Life

I t's pretty obvious that those with high EQ and a positive mindset live on a whole other level from everyone else. Their habits, behavior, the way they talk, the way they express themselves, there's something distinctively different that they do which set them apart from the crowd. Rising each morning and choosing to live life positively is how they remain motivated to keep doing what they do, to keep on succeeding and keep their success flowing.

If you want to start living a more positive life, take a look at the 15 qualities below that are often displayed by individuals with high emotional intelligence and a positive mindset. If you aspire to live a more positive life just like they do, then it's time to start doing what they do:

. . .

15 Traits of People Who Live a Positive Life

Individuals who live a positive life each day are always optimistic. They're hopeful, passionate, creative and in everything that they do, they give it their full effort without any complaints or cynicism in the mix. They always see the glass as half full, despite what everyone else thinks, and it is precisely this optimistic, happy, positive outlook of life that has driven them to achieve success where so many have failed to do so.

Let's take a look at some of the top 15 traits of people who make it a habit to live a positive life:

- They are focused on achieving their goals, and they never let any challenge defeat them or bring them down. They've always got a smile on their face, no matter how many setbacks they face, and they always stand up, brush themselves off and keep moving forward one step at a time.

- They live a happier, more satisfied life. They are grateful for everything that they have, and they make it a point to stop and appreciate life and everything that they've been given, which is why they're always happier than everyone else.

- They have more self-discipline than others because they view discipline in an optimistic way. Where others might see self-discipline as a burden having to sacrifice a lot of things that they're not happy about doing, a person with a positive outlook never sees it as a burden. They see it instead as a step that must be taken to bring them one step closer to where they want to be.

- They enjoy overcoming challenges because it is like a personal accomplishment to them. To overcome something difficult, something which pushed them out of their comfort zone and tested their boundaries, and still emerging victorious on the other side with a smile on their face is what keeps a positive thinking person going.

- They live in the present moment. They never look

back and dwell on past mistakes, because they
know it isn't going to bring them any benefit.
Instead, they live in the now and enjoy the present
opportunities that they have because they know it is
preparing them for a better future at hand.

- They're not afraid to push their boundaries because
  they are confident in themselves and their abilities.
  They are optimistic, and constantly tell themselves
  they are capable of doing anything that they set
  their mind to.

- They live a life that is free from the constraints of
  worrying about what other people think. They
  never let themselves be worked up or bothered by
  what other people think about them, and that's
  how they manage to live their life with such positive
  energy. They don't let the negative perceptions of
  others cloud their judgment.

- They are more successful in achieving their goals
  because you'll never find the words *I can't...* in the

vocabulary of someone who has a positive mindset about them. They always believe they are capable of absolutely anything, and it is that belief and that confidence in themselves that fuels them towards success.

- The respect and accept themselves for who they are. They don't need anyone else's opinions to feel validated. They don't focus on whether people like them or not, because they're more focused on building themselves up and creating a version of themselves that they like and respect. When they can look in the mirror and feel happy with the person they see looking back at them, that's all they need to go through the day with a smile on their face and a happy, positive outlook of life.

- They focus more on just getting things done, instead of focusing on how talented they are, or how good they may be at something. Even if they may not be the best, what matters to them is that they at least try to get things done. They are realistic, and they know that nobody can be the best at everything all the time, which is why they never use it as an excuse to hold themselves back.

- They read a lot. There's a lot to be learned between the pages of the book, which is why the successful individuals make it a habit of reading on a regular basis. They read books which inspire, motivate, empower and re-energize them, or give them ideas about what their next move towards success should be. The books that they read help them put things into perspective, which is why they manage to maintain the constant optimistic outlook towards life, even when they struggle.

- They make it a point to focus on the opportunities. Positive and high EQ people are always on the lookout for what their next move could be. The next step that is going to elevate their status just one step higher. They view everything which happens to them as an opportunity to either learn from or take advantage of.

- They actively avoid negativity like a plague. If there ever was an emotion that is so toxic it could completely unravel your life if you let it take control, it's negativity which is why positive minded and high EQ individuals avoid it like a plague and slam the door shut on that emotion. The minute they allow negativity into their lives, they know, it's only a matter of time before things could start to spiral, which is why they actively work at avoiding it and staying far away from it.

- They don't let the fear emotion overcome them and give into it. If you let your life be run by fear, you're always going to be held back and miss the opportunities that come your way. High EQ and positive minded people know this, which is why even though they may be afraid, they never let it stop them from making a big move and taking risks. They know that it is important to try at least, or you'll never know what could have been.

- They live a nutritious life. High EQ and positive minded individuals keep their mind sharp, and their body fit by eating a well-balanced diet which meets all their nutritional needs. They steer clear of anything which is going to impact their body negatively or prevent them from thinking clearly or impact their judgment. They keep themselves well-fed because they know how easy it is to become emotional when your body is running low on nutrition, especially when you're hungry. A well-balanced diet is a key to a happy, healthy mind.

Creating Your Perfect Environment for Success

Success is attributed to several variables, some which you can control, and some which you can't. Having determination, willpower and emotional intelligence on your side are some examples the variables which are within your control. Having a little bit of luck on your side and the right opportunity at the right time are examples of variables which you cannot control.

There is one thing that you can do, however, which ensures that your environment is always one that is conducive to success. An environment which always fosters positivity, making you want to live your best life every day. Having the mental attitude to want to live a life full of positivity alone is not enough, you need to build and create an environment which also stimulates you to do so. Our external environments have some degree of influence over the state of our minds. If we are in a surrounding which is dank, dark and downright depressing, it makes it very hard to have a positive outlook. Compare that to an environment which is bright, open, warm, inviting and cozy. Obviously, the latter scenario is the one where we'll find it much easier to live a more positive life because the environment has been designed to foster that success.

Your thoughts and behavior will be influenced to some degree by the environment which you surround yourself with daily because this is where you spend most of your time. An environment that increases productivity and allows freedom of expression is a great place to spend your time in as it will motivate and inspire you. A conducive environment keeps your positivity going, making it easier to live life with a happy, healthy, positive outlook every day. With the right kind of environment, you're less likely to be influenced by negative elements because you'll be so happy with what you have going on right now that you're not willing to let anything disrupt that happiness.

Here's how you can create an environment that encourages you to live a more positive life every day:

- **Stick Motivational Quotes Around Your Home -** Quotes, sayings, and mantras which encourage your development of a higher EQ are an excellent addition to your home or work space. Find a quote you like, get it printed out in whatever color you want and stick it right next to your goals that you have written down. With these bright, colorful quotes all around your home and office cubicle, they'll be hard to miss, and they'll serve as constant positivity reminders.

- **Have a Vision Board -** Another great element which encourages and fosters a positive mindset is to have a vision board with appealing imagery that is related to all the goals and desires you want to achieve. Use bold designs and vibrant colors, images which are your mind is attracted to. The minute you look at these pictures, you should feel a burst of happiness, have a smile on your face and feel infused with the right kind of positive energy. A vision board is especially great to have in the workspace because this is where you spend most of your time in each day. It can be easy to lose your motivation when your workspace is just a dull, uninspiring cubicle which seems to do nothing for you. But you can create a little positivity paradise of your own.

- **Have a Daily To-Do List** – Where important tasks always come first. That's how you ensure you remain productive throughout the day. Establishing a routine for yourself will make you much more productive. A routine allows you to get right down to the tasks that need to be done for the day, makes you more efficient because you know what needs to be done for the day without having to think too much about it, minimizes the time you need to spend on planning and helps to create structure in your life as well as instil good, productive habits when you do something in repetition.

Now is the time to start thinking positive and start building your confidence one step at a time. Remember that nobody else can do this for you, so it is up to you to start.

6

Understanding the Importance of Self

The importance of self can encompass several different aspects. Self-worth, self-esteem, self- awareness, and self-regulation, all of which are equally important in your quest for better emotional intelligence. Having a strong sense of self is a pivotal tool which you need to become someone who has high EQ successfully. Especially in today's world where it is so easy to let the hecticness and the constant stress make us lose touch with who we are.

Defining a Strong Sense of Self

A strong sense of self here is defined as the way that you perceive yourself. How big your belief in yourself is? When you have a strong sense of self, you're more confident, ambitious, determined and focused on what you want to get out of your life. Your belief in yourself is so strong that nothing can waver your confidence, and you don't need validation from anyone else to assure you of what you're capable of. That is what it means to have a strong sense of self.

Let's do a quick exercise here for a minute to determine where your current sense of self is:

- Do you love the person that you are right now?
- How much do you value yourself right now?
- Can you name 5 of your best qualities which you see as strengths?
- If you had to lead a group of people right now, would you be able to do it?

To increase your confidence, that sense of belief in yourself has to come from within you. That is where it all begins. No amount of external sources will be able to give you the level of confidence you desire if you don't believe in yourself, to begin with. The support and encouragement that you receive from others are just a bonus, to give you that extra bit of reassurance that you did do a good job. However, it is what you think that matters more, not what they say. If you constantly rely on others for validation, you're never going to be fully satisfied, and you'll constantly be searching for something more because it never seems to be enough.

A strong sense of self is going to be a crucial tool that you need as you work on improving your EQ levels. Self-awareness and self-regulation are the first two out of the five major principles which make up what emotional intelligence is. Self-awareness is going to require that you be connected with and attuned to who you are. What are your strengths, weaknesses, what emotional triggers set you off, how well you're able to cope with them, and how confident you are in handling the different situations that come your way? Self-regulation is then going to focus on how well you manage and control these emotional episodes when they occur. How well you're able to cope under pressure. How well you manage, yourself is going to be one of the most important things you do as you work on developing your emotional intelligence. EQ is going to require a high sense of self, and the belief in yourself to pull it off.

Why Having a Strong Sense of Self Matters

Although emotional intelligence isn't a subject you're going to find being taught in schools, it is one of the most important things that a person can learn, and it has a strong connection with your sense of self. When you've got high EQ, your relationships are healthier, you control your emotions instead of it controlling you, and it infuses you with a strong, healthy sense of self-esteem.

Life can be a real challenge, one that is full of surprises, some of which can take you on an emotional roller coaster. In the moments where you experience emotional turmoil or discomfort, having a strong sense of self is the inner strength that is going to help you see it through. Having a strong sense of self does not necessarily mean you're immune to experiencing emotional upheaval, it just means that you react differently than you normally would, especially when high EQ is involved in the mix. With a strong sense of self, your inner strength is the one that is going to help you self-regulate, soothe and calm yourself in the emotional moments when you need it the most.

Having a strong sense of self matters because:

- It enhances your level of self-awareness (high EQ) and knowledge about yourself. You know what your values, your beliefs, your strengths, and your weakness are and how to use them to your advantage.

- It makes self-acceptance easier. You stop trying to be someone that you're not, and you accept yourself wholeheartedly, including both the good and the bad. You acknowledge what your talents are, and you're perfectly fine admitting which areas might need some improvement. You accept that you're not 100% perfect, and that's okay.

- You're more confident affirming your boundaries. You no longer succumb to the pressure always to please others, because you realize that is something which can be detrimental and damaging to your sense of self. You are willing to compromise for the relationships that matter, but not to the extent where it violates your boundaries and affects your sense of self. This is how you maintain control of your emotions and avoid feeling overwhelmed or pressured into doing things you don't want to do.

- You take responsibility for your actions, which is what a good leader does. Wherever you go, people will look to you for guidance and leadership, because of the strong sense of self that you've got. Your strong sense of self guides your every decision and choice that you'll be displaying leadership qualities without even realizing it.

- You no longer have such strong emotional reactions to the things which are being said to you. That's because you know what you are worth, and when you know someone is saying something about you that isn't true, why let yourself get emotional about it? A strong sense of self makes you more accepting and attuned to the kind of person that you are, and that what others say about you does not define who you are in any way.

- It makes you comfortable with knowing when to say no. Sometimes, as much as you would like to help, it simply isn't worth it if it is going to affect your mental and physical health by doing so. Knowing when to say no comes from having a strong sense of self, because you know your limits and what you're capable of, and you don't feel pressured into agreeing just because you're worried about offending the person who asked for a favor.

Increase Your Sense of Self by Setting Yourself Free

If your sense of self is not where you want it to be right now, ask yourself why that is? What is holding you back? Do you constantly worry about the opinions of others? Are you worried if your actions are being judged? If you are, then it is time to set yourself free and reclaim your sense of self once more.

People with high emotional intelligence live a happier, more fulfilled life, one where they are always in control because they do not themselves be bothered by the judgments and opinions of others. They know that if they were to get all worked up and let it bother them, their emotions could quickly spiral out of control, their self-esteem gets affected and they find themselves taking several steps back instead of progressing forward the way that they should. Think about the last time that you were so worked up and bothered about what someone said about you. You spent weeks dwelling on it, and because it festered in your mind for so long, your sense of self was affected before you even realized what was happening.

Having high EQ means you need to believe in yourself enough and be confident in your own decisions and choices not to care what others may think. As long as you know, the course of action you chose is the right one for you at that time, believe that you made the decision that was best. Allowing yourself to constantly care about whether others are going to approve of your decision or not is just trapping yourself in an emotional prison. It is a restrictive and unhealthy thought pattern that has been holding you back all this time and messing with your emotions, causing you to obsess and worry over unnecessary things.

Reclaim your sense of self once more by reminding yourself that the only opinion that matters here is yours. This is your life, and you're the one who's living it, making choices and decisions which you have to live with. Your opinions, and the opinions of the people who matter (like family and friends who genuinely care about you), are the only thoughts that should matter. The people who care about you will always want only what's best for you. They will lift you, be supportive and build up your confidence because they care about seeing you succeed.

Don't let the opinions of others affect the way that you see yourself. When someone thinks or has anything negative to say about you, it is a reflection on them, not you. If you allow yourself to give in to your emotions because of what they say, it is going to eat away at your sense of self and diminish your confidence over time. Someone else's opinion can only matter if you allow it to matter.

7

Becoming an Effective and Aware Leader

Being a leader is a position which commands huge responsibility. All eyes are constantly on you. When a challenge or conflict arises, you're the one people turn to for solutions and answers. It is a big responsibility to oversee and manage a team of people, and the pressure to perform, to ensure that things are always running smoothly, rests on your shoulders.

No team, project or organization can succeed without good leadership leading the way which is why emotional intelligence is so important. When you've got so much on your plate to deal with, you're bound to go through all sorts of emotions. If you don't learn to manage and control those emotions, they're going to overwhelm you easily. Being a leader, and being an *effective* leader, are two very different things. The latter is the one that is destined for success.

Managing a company alone is overwhelming, but being an effective leader to a team of people who are the backbone of your company is an even more overwhelming task. You must be an effective leader if you're going to bring out the best in the people that you work with. A leader needs to constantly evaluate their leadership method to see if their approaches are working as well as they should.

Part of being an effective manager is knowing the strengths and weaknesses of your team members, and what each person brings to the table. This part can be achieved through the social skills, motivation and empathy part of the emotional intelligence core principles. An effective leader will never turn a blind eye to conflict and will do everything in their power to address the conflict as soon as it happens. To do this, you need to effectively tune into the emotions of the people who are involved in the conflict. Empathize with them, see where they're coming from. During conflict is when emotions tend to run high, and if you're not able to properly manage your own emotions, you won't be able to manage the emotions of others.

How to Become an Effective and Aware Leader

An effective leader is one that is not afraid of a challenge. Effective leadership is also not about bossing people around. It isn't just about telling them what to do. Effective leadership is about bringing out all the best qualities in all the people you work it, to get a team of people working together like a well-oiled machine. An effective leader breeds success. Effective leaders share in the responsibility and the workload of the team. They're not afraid to get down and dirty with the team, being one with the rest of them and taking on jobs that everyone else is doing.

As an effective leader, the responsibility also lies with you to let your team know you're always there for them no matter what. You need to let your people know that they matter to you. You need to nurture them, encourage them to grow in their way, empathize and be compassionate when you see that they are struggling. Emotional intelligence is your secret weapon to bringing out the best in your employees because it can help you connect with them in ways you couldn't imagine. This isn't just another boss-employee relationship. To be considered an *effective* and successful leader, you need to go the extra mile and look beyond that.

How do you use emotional intelligence to foster effective leadership and become more aware? By employing the following techniques:

- **Let Your Team Know They Matter -** People are emotional creatures. As a leader, if you want to be successful and effective, it is your job to listen to everyone's, and what they have to say. Make it your policy to encourage everyone to approach you and give them a chance to express themselves. Let them know they can come and talk to you about how they feel without judgment. Your job is to be encouraging, to empathize with them and make them feel supported. To make them feel like they matter.

- **Be Someone Who's Trustworthy -** You need to cultivate an environment of trust at all times when you are with their team. When a team can trust each other, they work much better together. When they know without a doubt, they can put their full trust in their leader to always have their best interest at heart, that makes for a happier, more positive team all around.

- **Forging Strong Connections -** Use the self-awareness and social skills aspect of emotional intelligence to help you foster stronger connections between you and the people you manage. Don't just connect for the sake of doing so, but build a connection that is meaningful, that shows the team members you genuinely care about them and their welfare. Reach out to them on a regular basis, congratulate them when they successfully meet their targets. Catch up with them regularly and talk about common interests. Ask them about their families, their hobbies, their passion. Build a relationship outside of just work matters.

- **Show Empathy -** There's a reason why this is one of the core principles of emotional intelligence. The people in your team have emotions and feelings, put yourself in their shoes and try to imagine what they would be feeling. This makes it much easier for you to see things from their perspective, to understand where they're coming from and why they're feeling the way that they do. An effective leader is one who can practice empathy and compassion with sincerity.

- **Listen Attentively -** When having a one-on-one conversation with a member of your team, listen to their voice inflections and the tone of their voice. Pay attention to the words they use, the points they emphasize on. Listen to the way they sound when they talk about how they feel. Self-awareness is what you need in this case. Practicing self-awareness (another EQ core principle) and listening attentively will help you connect with your people, and be empathetic towards them. It will help you be compassionate, understanding and nurturing in all the ways that they need.

- **Be Mutually Respectful -** Respect and encourage respect among every single person in the organization and team, because everyone has a role to play and their role contributes to the overall success. The most effective type of leaders are ones that provide a work environment where employees help each other and value the contributions that each makes. This can only be achieved by mastering emotional intelligence because without the crucial self-awareness, motivational and social skills needed, you're going to find it very hard to manage yourself and everyone else.

- **Take Time to Reflect On Your Feelings -**
  Leaders are sometimes so busy looking after
  everyone else that they forget to check in with
  themselves and their feelings. Part of being an
  effective leader with high levels of emotional
  intelligence is about being able to check in with
  yourself now and then. What have your feelings
  been lately? Reflect on them for several moments.
  This helps to avoid you falling out of touch with
  yourself and everyone else around you. Leaders
  have a lot on their plate, and they can be so busy
  trying to manage everything else that they forget
  stopping to take care of themselves is something
  they need to do.

- **Taking Breaks When You Need It -** Leaders
  are always expected to bring their A-game and be
  switched on all the time. It is easy to forget that
  leaders are people too, with feelings and emotions.
  They too, like everyone else, can burn out if they
  fail to take care of themselves. They too can be
  easily drained by having to manage all sorts of
  emotions. The emotionally intelligent thing to do is
  to stop and take breaks whenever you need them. It

is perfectly okay to take some time to recharge your batteries. In fact, you should make it a point to do this to keep you drowning in your own emotions. Being a leader is challenging, and it can take a toll on you emotionally, mentally and physically. Whenever you think you need a break to recharge, take it and don't feel guilty about doing so.

As a leader with huge amounts of responsibility on your shoulders, you *need* emotional intelligence to help you sort through your feelings in healthy ways. Emotional intelligence teaches you how to regulate your impulses, so you don't act out emotionally and in the heat of the moment, because that's not what an effective leader does. That's how your people end up losing trust in you if you appear to be a leader who is unpredictable and acts out emotionally. EQ does make a *big difference* in the level of success you achieve because it trains you to focus on what matters. It teaches you to remain calm, focused and in control in the moments when you need it most. More importantly, it teaches you how to get a handle on the negative emotions that could threaten to disrupt your success. It teaches you to be mindful and to be attuned to the way that you're feeling at crucial moments. That is how emotional intelligence helps you become a more effective and aware leader.

8

The Art of Effective Communication

B esides a high level of EQ, there is one other quality that everyone should possess to help them thrive in the work environment and everyday life in general. That quality is effective communication. You could have all the most brilliant ideas, the best strategies and the best plans for success, but if you don't know how to communicate those ideas effectively, they are not going to be of much use to you. Even in everyday life, if you struggle to communicate, it can be a real challenge. It can be very stressful trying to get people to understand what you're trying to say and where you're coming from.

Which is why the art of effective communication is something you need to work on improving, along with your emotional intelligence. For communication to be considered effective and successful, your message must be understood clearly. The exchange of information that goes on between two or several individuals must be clearly understood by all involved, with little or no misunderstandings happening.

Why Effective Communication Matters

How often have you thought about the way that you communicate? Give it some serious thought for a minute. Communication is a skill that many don't think twice about, but it is one of the most important skills you could have at your disposal. Effective communication matters because it helps us relate and collaborate with the people living in the world with us.

Effective communication is also important because:

- **It Avoids Misunderstandings -**
  Misunderstandings increase the chances of conflict. This often happens when information is misconstrued or taken out of context. Why does this happen? Because there's a lack of effective communication going on. Misunderstandings can often lead to heated arguments, fights and severed relationships depending on the seriousness of the situation. If you have ever gone for weeks, months

or maybe even years without speaking to someone because of a misunderstanding, you'll know exactly just how damaging this can be. Which further emphasizes why it is so important that we all work on improving our communication skills. We communicate with hundreds of people throughout our lives, every day and in the workplace. You need to be able to express your messages clearly so that it minimizes the chances that what you're going to say is going to cause problems for yourself and the people that you're speaking to.

- **It Helps You Form Powerful Relationships -** The connections that we make in life matter, especially in the career world. In fact, how well you're able to connect to other people is the foundation of all relationships. Everyone starts as strangers in the beginning, and it is through communication that those bonds are taken to another level. People start talking; you get to know each other, form connections based on mutual interest. All of this can only happen if you're able to express yourself well through effective communication. If nobody can understand what you're trying to say, it makes it harder to connect to you. For example, think of a time when you tried to forge a connection with someone who didn't speak the same language. Wasn't it much harder? That's a struggle you would have to deal with on a regular basis without the power of effective communication.

- **It Boosts Your Confidence -** Successful leaders and individuals alike seem to ooze confidence on every level. When they speak, people stop and listen, transfixed by what they're saying. When they speak, people absorb what they're saying, which is how they manage to captivate large groups of audiences. That's the art of effective communication at work. When you're able to communicate effectively, your confidence level is given a tremendous boost because you do not doubt at all that you can express and tell people exactly what you want them to know. You find that you are no longer shy and awkward when it comes time for you to speak because you exactly know what to do and how to handle the situation. You know exactly what needs to be done. Success cannot be achieved if you're not able to convey yourself properly. If you're going to be a leader who is able to command large groups of people, the people must be able to understand you effortlessly.

- **It Gives You a Leg Up In Your Career -** Our workplace is where we spend the majority of our day. From Monday right up to Friday, morning to evening, our lives are focused on our careers and doing our jobs. If you aspire to achieve great heights in your career, effective communication, and emotional intelligence is the winning combination that you need. In the workplace, communication skills are just as vital as all the other skill sets you need to get your job done right. Without it, it's only a matter of time before you get overtaken by those with better communication abilities. Effective communication can give you a leg up in your career because it helps you form and maintain relationships, build rapport with the people who matter. It enables you to work cohesively with people from various departments and diverse backgrounds. It helps you effectively handle both easy and difficult clients, and even challenging situations. In the career world, it is all about how productive you are, and whether you're viewed as an asset to the company or the job that is going to put you ahead of everyone else. With a high EQ and effective communication skills at your disposal, you're already on your way to becoming a winner.

- **It Helps Promote Teamwork and Innovation at the Workplace -** When you're comfortable enough to communicate your ideas at work freely, it helps to increase the level of innovation experienced. This, in turn, increases the chances of good ideas and contributions being implemented at work to improve the workflow, draw in new clients and improve the company's daily operations as a whole. When effective communication flows freely in the workplace, it is easier to build teams which are productive and cohesive, who work well together to get things done. When colleagues and different teams are able to come together, work well and communicate effectively with each other, staff morale is given a boost, and there's generally a more positive vibe and feel at work. Instead of dreading your job, you might even come to love it because you feel productive, and you know that you're making contributions that are only serving to improve your reputation as an employee.

Communication Barriers You Need to Overcome

For effective communication to take place, you're going to need to overcome the barriers that are preventing it from happening. Communication is complex. Sometimes, despite all your efforts, misunderstandings could still occur. During the communication process, there are sometimes barriers which tend to come up that can result in poor communication. These are communication barriers.

These barriers are the reason your messages tend to become misconstrued or taken out of context. Some examples of communication barriers include:

- **Information Overload** - Not everyone processes information in the same way. If you distribute your information too fast and too soon, you could risk overwhelming the person you're speaking to because they don't have enough time to process what you're telling them.

- **Language Differences -** The world we live in today is more diverse than it has ever been. We come into contact with people from all sorts of different cultural backgrounds. While this is a wonderful thing, the different languages and accents can sometimes prove to be a communication barrier. Some words may be pronounced differently, or sentences become difficult to understand because of a different accent.

- **Being Distracted by External Factors -** Our mobile phones are perhaps the biggest distraction in our lives. General noise, other people talking, phones ringing, traffic honking, messages beeping into your mobile phone, even the urge to frequently check social media is a communication barrier because it distracts you from focusing on the message that you should be receiving.

- **Making Assumptions** - We've all been guilty of jumping to conclusions even before the person we're talking to has finished what they're trying to say. This barrier occurs when you decide to reach on a course of action without fully listening to all the information first. When you make assumptions, you're mentally blocking out the rest of the message without even realizing it, tuning out and not paying attention anymore because you've already jumped ahead to what you think should be done next. You run the risk of making even more mistakes this way.

- **A Lack of Self-Confidence -** Being shy and nervous can be viewed as a communication barrier because it makes the communication awkward. When you're shy, you tend to mumble, stutter or even forget a lot of what you intended to say.

- **Talking in A Hurry -** Rushing through the message puts you at risk of missing crucial information which needs to be communicated. When you speak in the hurried manner, you could stress out the person you're speaking to because they can't keep up with what you're trying to say.

How to Improve Your Communication Skills

To start working on becoming a more effective communicator, here is what you need to start working on and taking into account:

- **Go Right to the Point -** Being concise and specific is the best way to get your message across in the most effective manner. Communicate only the essential points, and leave out anything that is unnecessary. People have short attention spans, and this technique is the best way to ensure all the important information is conveyed the way that it should be.

- **Focus on the Message -** Stay focused on the message. The more focused you are on what's important, the better you are able to ensure that the important information is clearly communicated with minimal room for misunderstanding. For example, at the workplace, if you were talking about a co-worker's performance, focus on the performance aspect alone and avoid discussing unrelated matters such as their personality or the way they are dressed as an example.

- **Keep Distractions at Bay -** If you know you're about to have an important conversation, put away anything that can serve as a distraction. Put your mobile phone on silent, put it away in your pocket, find a quiet space where you can speak. Do your best to give the person your full attention and request that they do the same.

- **Be an Active Listener -** Effective communication is not just about you speaking and making yourself heard, it is about learning to be an active listener too. Communication works both ways, and for both parties to fully benefit from the conversation, you must be an equally active listener. This is where the social skills and the empathy aspect of emotional intelligence come into play because you need to be attuned to the emotions and feelings of people around you too.

- **Speak with Clarity -** Speak clearly and confidently, and pronounce each word clearly. Avoid meek, soft tones and especially avoid mumbling or muttering your words because nobody will be able to understand what you're saying when you do.

Whether it is in your personal life or your workplace, there is no denying that communication is one of the most important skills you can develop. Great communication skills can make a world of difference. Your success in life is dependent on how well you can regulate your emotions, and your ability to effectively communicate well with others. This is how you build successful relationships. When you combine those skills with the emotional intelligence techniques you learned in the earlier chapters, there's going to be nothing holding you back from success after this.

Conclusion

Thank for making it through to the end of this book, let's hope it was informative and able to provide you with all of the tools you need to achieve your goals whatever they may be.

Your emotions guide every choice, every decision and every step that you make in life. As your self-awareness increases, you will slowly begin to notice it whenever you're faced with a choice to make. The good news is, you're now equipped with everything you need to know about what it takes to become a more emotionally intelligent person.

As you move forward from here and make the necessary changes needed to improve your EQ, use the strategies, tips, and techniques which you've gathered from this book as you see fit. The tools are here to help you, and you should use them in a way that works best for you. No matter what your ultimate goal may be for your emotional intelligence, this guidebook is here to help you every step of the way.

This is going to be a journey that's going to take time to see the changes manifest itself visibly in your life, so don't get discouraged or frustrated. You are progressing forward, even if you think you're not. Take it slow, pace yourself and don't rush. Take this time to work on strengthening yourself emotionally from within. Practice the strategies in your life every day, and eventually, you will get there. If it helps, focus on mastering one technique at a time before you move onto the next one.

Building and mastering your EQ is something which you will gain over time. It is a skill, a technique and a piece of knowledge which must be carefully honed, crafted and culti-vated. Setbacks will happen along the way, but take them as learning curves, a challenge to overcome that is just going to make you better in the end. Most of all, be kind and patient with yourself. You're starting something incredible just by taking these first few steps towards improving your EQ. Whenever you need some help, you always have this guide-book to turn back to. Every tip and technique in here is meant to help you along with your process, so fully utilize it to your advantage.

Finally, if you found this book useful in any way, a review on Amazon is always appreciated!

Lightning Source UK Ltd.
Milton Keynes UK
UKHW020650140321
380284UK00005B/484